CW00858064

To read fluently is one of the basic aims of anyone learning English as a foreign language. **And it's never too early to start.** Ladybird Graded Readers are interesting but simple stories designed to encourage children between the ages of 6 and 10 to read with pleasure.

Reading is an excellent way of reinforcing language already acquired, as well as broadening a child's vocabulary. Ladybird Graded Readers use a limited number of grammatical structures and a carefully controlled vocabulary, but where the story demands it, a small number of words outside the basic vocabulary are introduced. In *The Magic Stone* the following words are outside the basic vocabulary for this grade:

fit for a king, poor, onion, tramp, turnip

Further details of the structures and vocabulary used at each grade can be found in the Ladybird Graded Readers leaflet.

A list of books in the series can be found on the back cover.

British Library Cataloguing in Publication Data

Ullstein, Sue
  The magic stone.
  I. Title   II. Aitchison, Martin
  428.6'4
  ISBN 0-7214-1212-2

First edition

Published by Ladybird Books Ltd Loughborough Leicestershire UK
Ladybird Books Inc Auburn Maine 04210 USA

© LADYBIRD BOOKS LTD MCMLXXXIX
All rights reserved. No part of this publication may be reproduced, stored in a retrieval system, or transmitted in any form or by any means, electronic, mechanical, photo-copying, recording or otherwise, without the prior consent of the copyright owner.
Printed in England

The Magic Stone

written by Sue Ullstein
illustrated by Martin Aitchison

Ladybird Books

This is a tramp. He wants to see
the world. But he has no money,
so he walks from town to town.
It is evening. He is tired
and hungry.

"I must stop soon," he says.
"I'm tired and hungry."

He walks on. He is looking for
a house. But there are no houses
in the forest. There are
only trees.

The tramp sees an old woman.
She is getting wood
for her fire.

"She has a kind face,"
the tramp thinks.

"Good evening," the tramp
says. "What are you doing
in the forest?"

"I'm getting wood
for my fire," the old woman says.
"And what are you doing here?"
she asks. "Where are
you going?"

"I'm seeing the world,"
the tramp says. "But I'm tired.
I'm looking for a house for
the night. But there are
no houses in the forest."

"You can't come home
with me," the old woman
says. "There are no
houses in the forest.
You must sleep under
a tree. Goodbye."

The tramp follows the old woman.

"Can't you help me?" he asks.
"Please take me home with you.
I'll go away tomorrow
morning."

The tramp and the old woman
go on.

Then the old woman says, ''You can sleep in my house for one night. But there isn't a bed for you. You must sleep on a chair.''

"Thank you, thank you,"
the tramp says.

They walk to the old woman's
house.

"I am tired and hungry,"
the tramp says.

"I can't give you any food,"
the old woman says. "I am poor.
I haven't any food."

They go into the old woman's
garden. The tramp looks
at the garden. He sees
onions and turnips. There is
a cow, too.

''Good,'' the tramp thinks.
''This old woman has some
food. I can have a good
supper here.''

The old woman and the tramp go
into the house.

"Sit down," the tramp says.
"Let me help you. You're hungry
and I'm hungry. Let me make
you some soup."

"Soup?" the old woman says.
"How can you make soup?
There isn't any food in
the house."

"I can do a lot of things,"
the tramp says. "I can make
soup from a stone."

"Soup from a stone?" the old woman says. "I must see this. Can I watch?"

"You are very kind," the tramp says. "You are letting me sleep here, so I'll let you watch."

The old woman sits down on a chair. She watches the tramp. He puts some water on the fire. Then he goes into the garden. He brings back a stone. He puts the stone into the water. He begins to stir the water and the stone. The old woman watches.

21

"Will the soup taste good?" the old woman asks.

"Yes, it will taste good," the tramp says. "Stone soup tastes better with an onion in it. But you haven't got any onions..."

He stirs the water with the stone in it.

"I think there are some onions in my garden," the old woman says. "I'll go and look."

She goes into the garden.

Soon she comes back with two big onions. She puts them into the water with the stone.

The tramp stirs the soup. The old woman watches.

"This soup will taste good,"
the tramp says. "Stone soup
tastes better with some meat
in it. But you haven't got
any meat..."

"I think there's some meat," the old woman says. "I'll go and look."

She goes out and soon she comes back with some meat. She puts it into the soup with the onions and the stone.

The tramp stirs the soup. The
old woman watches.

"This soup will taste good,"
the tramp says. "Stone soup
tastes better with some turnips
in it. But you haven't got
any turnips..."

"I think there are some
turnips in my garden,"
the old woman says.
"I'll go and look."

She goes into the garden.

Soon she comes back with
two big turnips.

The old woman puts them
into the soup with the meat,
the onions and the stone.

The tramp stirs the soup.
The old woman watches.

The old woman is hungry
now.

"That soup is good," she says.

"Yes, it is," the tramp says.
"Stone soup tastes
better with some milk in it. But
you haven't got any milk..."

"Yes, I have," the old woman says. "I have a cow. I'll get some milk from her."

The old woman goes out.

Soon she comes back with some milk.

She puts it into the soup with the turnips, the meat, the onions and the stone.

The tramp stirs the soup. The old woman watches.

The tramp tastes the soup.

"Is it good?" the old woman asks.

"Yes, it is," the tramp says. "But it needs some salt."

"I'll get some salt," the old woman says. She goes out.

Soon she comes back with some salt. She puts it into the soup with the milk, the turnips the meat, the onions and the stone.

The tramp stirs the soup. The old woman watches.

"Can we have the soup now?"
the old woman asks.

"Yes," the tramp says. "I'll
take out the stone. Then we can
have the soup. This soup is
fit for a king."

'But a king always has other
food, too,'' the old woman says.

And she puts a lot of good things
on the table.

'Now that's a supper fit for
a king,'' she says.

"Sit down," the tramp says.
"Taste the soup. Is it good?"

The old woman tastes the soup.

"Yes, it is," she says. "And
you made it from a stone!"

43

The tramp says, "You're very kind. You're letting me sleep here, so I'll give you the magic stone. You'll never be hungry again."

"Thank you, thank you," the old woman says. "You're very kind."

45

The old woman and the tramp
eat all the good food. They talk
and talk.

Then the old woman says, ''You're
very kind. You mustn't sleep
in a chair. You can sleep in
my bed. I'll sleep in a chair.''

So the tramp sleeps in the old woman's bed. The old woman sleeps in a chair by the fire.

47

The next day the tramp thanks the old woman.

"You mustn't thank me.
I must thank you.
You've given me the magic stone, so I'll never be hungry again," the old woman says.

"Come and see me again soon.
I'll make some soup for you."

"Yes, I will," the tramp says.
"Stone soup is good but you must
put in some onions, some meat,
some turnips and some milk, too!
Then put in some salt. You'll
have soup fit for a king!"

And he laughed!